For my wife and children. - NS

For my grandchildren. - MT

LITTLE SHOE PUBLISHING

Why Do We Eat Turkey on Thanksgiving?
Nicholas Scarpino
Copyright © 2020 by Nicholas Scarpino
All Rights Reserved

Illustrator: Marlene Turner
Editors: Mike Palmquist, Sarah Fabiny, Renae Scarpino
Cover and Interior Design: Tobi Carter

This book was self-published by the author, Nicholas Scarpino, under Little Shoe Publishing.
Published in the United States

ISBN 978-0-9891334-2-5 (paperback)
ISBN 978-0-9891334-3-2 (hardcover)
ISBN 978-0-9891334-4-9 (e-book)

Why Do We Eat Turkey on Thanksgiving?

Written by Nick Scarpino

Illustrated by Marlene Turner

Why do we eat **turkey** on Thanksgiving Day?
Why not **chicken** or **fish** or **steak**?
Did someone decide a long time ago?
Or is this tradition just one big mistake?

To learn more about Thanksgiving dinner,
Let's turn to someone who knows.
His name is **Hurkey the Turkey.**
He'll give us answers... Here goes!

The first Thanksgiving was in **1621**.
Plymouth, Massachusetts was the place
Pilgrims and Native Americans gathered
To thank God for His grace.

No one is sure if turkeys were served,
The meal was more likely **ducks** and **geese**.
Over three days and nights the group rejoiced
For their inaugural harvest feast.

Turkeys are native to America,
And were plentiful in the Pilgrims' day.
Our Founding Fathers loved eating turkey.
Would **George Washington** lead us astray?

In fact...

When Congress named the bald eagle
Our country's national bird,
Ben Franklin disagreed and said,
"EAGLES ARE LAZY . . . THAT'S ABSURD!"

The turkey is a **"bird of courage!"**
Franklin wrote to his daughter in a letter.
Thank you for the kind words, Mr. Franklin...
WE'RE SO GLAD YOU LIKE US BETTER!

For years we honored Thanksgiving
In many 'a different way.
Each state had its own celebration;
But there was **no national holiday.**

Turkey had not yet become
The star of Thanksgiving Day.
Perhaps in his book about Christmas
Charles Dickens helped pave its way.

After the ghosts paid **Scrooge** a few visits,
He sent a turkey to help **Bob Cratchit**.
Inspired by Scrooge, we Americans said,
A TURKEY... GREAT IDEA... LET'S MATCH IT!

UNITED STATES POST OFFIC

President of the united States

President Van Buren 1837
President Harrison 1841
President Tyler 1841
President Polk 1845
President Taylor 1849
President Fillmore 1850
President Pierce 1853
President Buchanan 1857
President Lincoln 1861

Now let's give **Sarah Josepha Hale**
Credit, thanks, and cheers.
She campaigned for a national holiday
For more than thirty years.

Mrs. Hale also wrote a book
That described a Thanksgiving dinner.
As for the dish at the head of the table...
Roasted turkey was the winner.

This country's Civil War
Was a storm we barely managed to weather.
President Lincoln named Thanksgiving
As a day to come together.

Our nation has observed Thanksgiving
Since the declaration from Lincoln.
That's 150 years and counting . . .
WOW! LET THAT SINK IN!

Ronald Reagan began a tradition
When he gave a **Presidential pardon**
To a turkey who was meant for dinner
But instead got to roam in the garden.

Today our Thanksgiving celebration includes
Parades with floats and marching bands,
Big balloons, performances,
And many people in the stands.

Runners rise at the crack of dawn
To compete in **turkey trots**.
Some folks volunteer to serve others,
Serving soup from steaming pots.

Football games take center stage.
They play from noon 'til night.
The winning teams get turkey legs,
And get to take a bite.

Well that concludes our history lesson,
And it's important to remember
There are many reasons we eat turkey
On the **fourth Thursday of November.**

But no matter what you choose to eat
For your Thanksgiving meal,
There are **some things more important**
We should celebrate with zeal.

Spending time with family and friends,
And **giving thanks to God,**
Are what Thanksgiving's all about,
And the things we should applaud.

Grandson Nick Scarpino and Grandmother Marlene Turner, pictured with Turner's original painting of Hurkey.

About the Author and Illustrator:

Marlene Turner has been an artist her entire life. She has painted portraits of each of her 15 grandchildren, crocheted blankets for each of her 22 great grandchildren, baked and created numerous wedding cakes, and illustrated a family cookbook. When she painted Hurkey the Turkey to serve as a Thanksgiving decoration, little did she know how much her family would love the painting. In fact, one of her grandchildren, Nick Scarpino, said he would write a book about Thanksgiving if his grandmother would illustrate it with drawings of Hurkey. At the age of 86, Turner drew the illustrations you see here to go along with Scarpino's story.

This grandmother and grandson team hope you learned something from this book, and that Hurkey brings your family as much joy as he has brought theirs.

CPSIA information can be obtained
at www.ICGtesting.com
Printed in the USA
LVHW071949291020
670161LV00017B/494